by

Joe Inglis

Illustrated by Graham Robson

Public Eye Publications

A Public Eye Publications Book

www.thegreatestintheworld.com

Illustrations:
Graham Robson, 'Drawing the Line'
info@dtline.co.uk

Cover design:
pentacorbig:
book & information graphic design
www.pentacorbig.co.uk

Layout design:
Bloomfield Ltd.

Copy editor:
Bronwyn Robertson
www.theartsva.com

Series creator / editor:
Steve Brookes

This first edition published in 2006 by
Public Eye Publications, PO Box 3182,
Stratford-upon-Avon, Warwickshire CV37 7XW

Text and Illustrations Copyright © 2006 - Public Eye Publications

'The Greatest in the World' Copyright © 2004 - Anne Brookes

A CIP catalogue record for this book is available from the British Library
ISBN 1-905151-10-1

Printed and bound by Biddles Books Limited, King's Lynn, Norfolk PE30 4LS

To my wonderful wife Jenny for all her love and support.

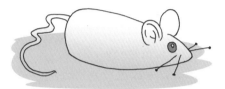

Contents

A few words from Joe Inglis . . .

People and cats have a long history of living together – from the ancient Egyptians right up to the modern day, man and cat have been pretty much inseparable. So surely, by now, we should have cats worked out - after 6000 years of cat ownership, surely there can't be much we don't know and understand about our feline friends?

Well, you would have thought so wouldn't you, but that doesn't seem to be the case at all. Cats still surprise us at every turn - whether they're suddenly biting the hand that strokes them, or mysteriously vanishing for days on end, cats seem to have an inbuilt ability to confuse and confound us humans. And it's not just everyday cat owners that can be mystified by cats - even seasoned cat professionals such as vets can end up being driven to despair. I remember one cat I used to own several years ago who developed a very strange habit which lead to all sorts of difficulties with my neighbours – he took to stealing children's cuddly toys from nearby houses and bringing them home to proudly lay at my feet!

It's from experiences like this – as well as looking after all my feline patients at work – that the tips in this book have come. From dealing with a kleptomaniac cat to getting the excess pounds of an overweight puss, there's advice for pretty much every feline eventuality. It's not designed as the definitive book on all aspects of cat care – it's more a resource for you to turn to as your life with your cat unfolds. For every stage of your cat's life there are tips and hints which should make his – and your – life better! Just don't forget the one most important tip though – never underestimate your cat, who'll always surprise you!

Good luck!

Joe

The Greatest Cat Tips in the World

1. The Patter of Tiny Feet

There's nothing like the patter of tiny feet to liven up your home – especially if they're furry and connected to an adorable little kitten! However before you make the decision to introduce a feline friend into your life, there's a lot to think about and consider. Here are my top tips for helping you work out if a cat is for you – and then finding the perfect 'purry' partner to fill your life!

Is a cat for you?

It might sound like the easiest decision you'll ever have to make – should I bring home this beautiful, cuddly kitten or not? But before you rush in, it's well worth taking a little while to think about how a cat is going to fit into your life.

Remember that cats can live for over twenty years, so bringing a kitten home is going to be the start of a very long relationship. And owning a cat is going to change your life in many ways – mainly for the better of course - but there are some changes which might take a bit of adjusting to. For example, you can't just drop everything and jet off on holiday when you own a cat, as you need to make sure he will be properly cared for while you're away. And what about the impact a cat will have on your house – cat hair and scratched sofas are par for the course when it comes to owning a cat!

So my tip is to take your time and make sure you are ready to commit to a cat – and then once you've made up your mind, and you're sure you're ready to share your life with a cat, it's time to get out there and choose the one for you!

Five things to think about before you get a cat!

Just as a quick check, to really, really make sure you are ready for a cat, have a look at my top five things to think about and make sure you are happy with all these things!

1. Cats are furry! Can you cope with the idea of cat fluff all round the house?

2. Cats eat smelly food! Are you happy to have a dish of cat food in the kitchen?

3. Cats catch mice! How would you feel if your cat dragged a half-eaten mouse into the living room?

4. Cats have claws! Are you prepared to have your finest sofa used as a scratching post?

5. Cats are wonderful! If you've got this far down the list and you agree with this, then you're definitely ready for a cat!

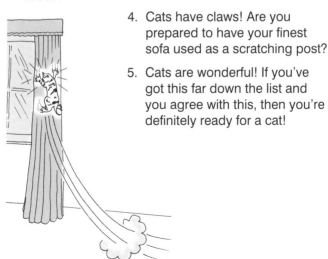

Taking on a stray cat

If a cat wanders into your life and decides that it would like to live with you, there are a few important things to consider before making the new arrival a permanent member of the household.

Firstly, you need to make sure that the cat really is a stray, and that it hasn't got an owner searching desperately for it while you feed it cream and pilchards! To do this, have a look for a tag if the cat is wearing a collar. If there is a tag, it should have a phone number for you to call. Don't be tempted to ignore the number – just imagine how you'd feel if it was your cat. If there isn't a tag, you should take the cat to your vet who will scan him for a microchip (as well as give him a thorough check over). Microchips are implanted under the skin of the scruff of the neck, and contain a unique number, which is used to identify the cat and reunite it with its owners.

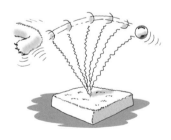

13

Kitten or cat?

Owning a kitten from a young age and watching her grow from a mischievous bundle of fluff into a full-grown adult cat is a wonderful experience – but it's not the only alternative if you want to own a cat. There are thousands of adult cats languishing in rescue centres across the country, and giving one of these poor cats a new home and a new life can be just as rewarding and enjoyable as bringing up a kitten. It's also a great option if you are elderly, as there are lots of older rescue cats waiting for new homes, and by taking in one of these, you can have all the pleasure of a cat but without the worry of owning a pet who might outlive you.

Top five places to look for a rescue cat

1. Your local branch of Cats Protection. Their website is www.cats.org.uk.

2. Local animal rescue charities – ask your vet for details.

3. Council-run pounds for stray cats and dogs – ask your local council.

4. The Blue Cross – a national charity which re-houses thousands of unwanted cats every year. Their website is www. bluecross.org.uk

5. On your doorstep!

A testing time . . .

One more tip if you're taking in a stray – get her checked for two of the most serious infectious diseases, feline leukaemia virus, and feline AIDS. Stray cats can pick up these viruses but not show any symptoms for many years, so it's really important to check your cat before taking her on. An infected cat could easily pass on the infection to other cats, and will need special care and attention throughout its life.

Finding the right kitten for you . . .

If your heart is set on a kitten, then you've got a bit of work to do! Firstly you need to make some important decisions about what kind of kitten you would like, and then think about how you are going to find this dream cat of yours!

Kittens come in many shapes, sizes and colour, and you should do some research about what kind of cat is going to suit your life the best. You might be happy with a good old moggy, or perhaps you'd prefer something a little more exotic like a Birman or Siamese. Or for those with really deep pockets and exotic tastes, there are the rare and beautiful breeds like the Bengal and Maine Coon.

Have a look through my breed tips in the next section to help you decide on what type of kitten to go for – and then carry on reading for my top tips about where to find your kitten.

Right kitten, wrong kitten!

So you've found a breeder, and there's a litter of gorgeous-looking kittens ready to go, but how do you know they're healthy – and how do you pick the right one? Well, follow these simple rules, and you should have no difficulty in picking a winner from the litter:

How big?

First, compare the sizes of the kittens, and try to avoid picking any that are much smaller than the others. This probably means they've not had a good start in life and they might be less healthy as a result (although saying that, someone's got to home the unwanted ones, so if you really fall for the runt of the litter, let your heart rule your head and take him home for a life of TLC!)

Get clinical!

Get your white coat on and give the litter a thorough examination, from tiny head to tail! Look at their eyes for discharges, their legs for deformities and take a peek in their mouths to make sure there are no cleft palates (a small hole in the roof of the mouth).

How to find your perfect kitten – in seven easy steps!

1. Buy a copy of a good cat magazine and head to the back pages – you'll find full listings of all the major breeders.

2. Pop in to your vet – most practices will know lots of breeders and individuals with kittens looking for homes.

3. Contact the Governing Council of the Cat Fancy which represents cat breeders. Their number is +44 (0)1278 427575 and their email is info@gccfcats.org

4. Take a trip to a cat show – the biggest is the Supreme Cat Show, which is held in the NEC, Birmingham in November every year. For more information visit www.supremecatshow.org.

5. Make contact with your local RSPCA office as they may know of a kitten that you could just fall in love with.

6. Visit the Cats Protection at www.cats.org.uk.

7. Ask at any local cat or animal shelter in case they are aware of someone who has a suitable kitten that needs a loving home.

How to spot an unhealthy kitten

- Worms – kittens with lots of intestinal worms will have a swollen pot belly and a dull coat, and might have worm segments around their bottom (yuk!).

- Fleas and flea-dirt in fur – look for tiny black specks on the back near the tail.

- Discharge from eyes or nose – this is a likely sign of cat flu.

- Shaking head with waxy ears – a sure-fire sign of ear mites.

- Matted fur around the back end – indicates chronic diarrhoea.

Did you know?

That some cats are born with extra toes – as many as seven on each foot! Cats with this condition are known as polydactyl meaning, literally, 'many toes'. The extra toes don't usually cause problems, but they are often surgically removed to prevent them catching on things.

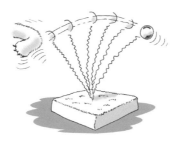

Psychoanalysis time!

You need to have a think about character – do you want the bossy kitten who marches to the front of the litter demanding attention? Or would you prefer the timid one who's waiting quietly at the back of the pack? Watch the litter playing and choose the character that most fits your idea of a cool cat.

The eye of the beholder

After personality, it's time to think about looks. If you're considering showing your new kitten then obviously his appearance is everything, and you'll need to check that all the markings and colours are just right. On the other hand, if your cat is destined for the sofa rather than the show ring, concentrate more on character than colour.

And finally . . .

. . . it's always worth remembering the most important tip of all – let your heart rule your head. You're going to be sharing your life with this cat, so you need to pick the kitten you really fall for.

Meet the parents . . .

One final tip when it comes to picking a kitten is to have a good look at the mother (and father if he's around). Certain pedigree cats have some extreme physical traits, such as Persians with very short noses that can cause serious health problems. Always go for cats bred with the health of the cat as the first priority, and steer clear of litters born to parents that are obviously in-bred and unhealthy.

The journey home

To carry your new kitten home, you need a good quality cat box. When you're buying the box, remember that your kitten will grow, so make sure it's sturdy enough to cope with a full-grown cat. The best boxes are made of plastic, as this is easy to clean, but watch out for cheap ones that have weak lids and tend to fall open (never a good thing, especially when you've spent hours getting the cat into the box ready for a trip to the vet!). If you can't get hold of a cat box, check out my next tip for a cunning alternative which is much cheaper – and you're bound to have the ingredients ready at home!

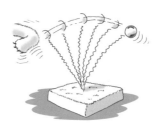

A study in
how the
size of a cat
INCREASES
the nearer it
gets to a
cat-basket . . .

A pillowcase makes a great cat carrier!

Now this might sound like a bizarre tip but believe me, pillowcases really do make great cat carriers! Cats seem to love being able to hide away inside, and you can hold them comfortably in your arms with little chance of them being able to easily escape. Just remember to take the cat out before you go to bed, or you could be in for a difficult night's sleep!

Welcome home puss!

Arriving in a new and strange home is a daunting experience for a young kitten, so it's worth making sure that her first few days are as stress free as possible. If you've got other pets, keep them out of the way for a couple of days, and then introduce them to the new arrival gradually and under supervision. If you've got children, don't let them overwhelm the kitten, and try to teach them to be calm and considerate with her.

Make sure there's a comfy cat bed waiting for her, preferably situated somewhere nice and quiet where she can escape all the other pets and people. And offer her a saucer of warmed milk and some tasty kitten food, along with a big bowl of clean water.

Some good news . . .

Now you've made that commitment and got yourself a lovely new cat, I've got some good news for you – owning a cat will statistically make you live longer! Research has shown that cat owners have lower blood pressure, less chance of suffering from a heart attack, and experience less stress than people without cats in their lives. So sit back, stoke the cat, and start planning for a long life together!

The Name Game!

One last thing you'll need to think about when you get a new cat is his or her name. Think carefully about this because whilst a funny or silly name might seem like a good idea now, just imagine how you'll feel in a crowded vet's waiting room when the vet calls out 'Fluffy Trixibell please'!

To help you out, here are the top ten cat names in the UK:

1. Sooty
2. Tigger
3. Lucy
4. Smokey
5. Charlie
6. Smudge
7. Thomas
8. Sam
9. Misty
10. Lucky

2. Joe's Top Ten Cat Breeds

Did you know that the first domestic cats were kept by the ancient Egyptians as long as 7,000 years ago? Since that time cats have always played an important role in human society, keeping mice and rats away from food stores – and, of course, providing companionship and affection.

Modern cats have changed over the centuries, shaped by selective breeding, so that now there are literally hundreds of varieties or breeds, ranging from the good old tabby moggy through to the rare and exotic show cats which have been bred exclusively for their unusual looks.

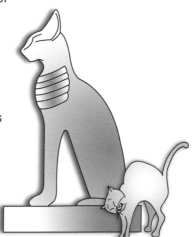

Here are a few facts and tips about the ten most popular and interesting cat breeds around today. If you're thinking about getting a pedigree cat, have a read through and see which one takes your fancy…

Abyssinian

One of the oldest know breeds and the ultimate cat for those looking for the sphinx-like Egyptian cat - the elegant feline with a muscular body, beautiful arched neck, large ears and almond shaped eyes. In fact some people think that these cats are directly descended from an ancient Egyptian breed. Whatever the truth about their origins, Abyssinians still retain the jungle look of the African wildcat - the ancestor of all domestic cats. These cats make good companions and generally live very long and healthy lives.

Not to be confused with . . . a rabbit! They all have a very distinctive 'ticked' coat which is caused by a mutant tabby gene, which makes their coat resemble a rabbit or hare!

Angora

These 'oriental' cats are the result of a strange breeding experiment in the 1960's involving an Abyssinian and a Siamese. They are longhaired, which means they require regular grooming, and can be a little noisy and inquisitive.

Angora cats are some of the most adorable pets around. People who own Angoras are always struck by the breed's ability to be amazingly adorable, young, and curious throughout their lives. A great feature on their faces is their eyes which can come in several different colours including amber, blue and a one orange, one blue combination. The fur of Angoras is known as being very silky and almost silvery. It's the fur of the Angoras that make them so soft and lovable.

Not to be confused with . . . Angora rabbits which produce the wool for Angora jumpers!

Bengal

This rare and exotic breed of cat looks like a miniature leopard, and is the product of a strange series of events involving an Asian leopard cat, a domestic moggy, and a Californian scientist in the 1960s! Despite these strange beginnings, the breed has quickly become very popular with owners looking for a touch of the wild cat in their pet, and it is the must-have breed for dedicated followers of cat fashion!

Even the voice of the Bengal is different from that of other domestic cats as they can coo and chirp. They also like to jump and somersault and love to play with water! The Bengal is self-assured, affectionate and playful, with the stunning looks of its wild ancestor.

Not to be confused with . . . a leopard kitten!

Birman

If you don't like cat fluff up your nose and white hairs all over your furniture, don't consider the Birman! These semi-longhaired cats, with beautiful cream-coloured fur and blazing blue eyes, can make great pets or show animals - as long as you're prepared for some regular grooming work. The Birman's personality, however, is marvellous - gentle, active, playful, but quiet and unobtrusive if you are busy with other things.

Did you know . . . Birmans are believed to be descended from sacred cats which lived in Burmese temples many centuries ago? They were thought to bring courage and peace to those around them - so well worth considering if you've got a house full of unruly children!

British Shorthair

The British Shorthair, probably the oldest English breed of cat, traces its ancestry back to the domestic cat of Rome. If there were ever to be a 'Pedigree Cat Boxing Championship', I think there is no doubt that the British Shorthair would come out on top! These cats are built like the proverbial brick litter tray, and have an air of undeniable toughness about them - but despite this, they are generally very friendly and easy going. A British Shorthair is always in quiet control of his or her environment, supervising everyone and everything that happens in the family. One to consider if you're scared of the neighbours but haven't got space for a Rottweiler...

Watch out for . . . too long a coat, a weak chin or overly fluffy tail if you want to show your British Shorthair, as the judges will pick on these features as 'faults'.

Cornish and Devon Rex

These two breeds from the West Country have one thing in common - a really weird curly coat, which has either no guard hairs (Cornish Rex) or soft guard hairs (Devon Rex). Both breeds came about as a result of genetic mutations which were noticed by keen cat fanciers, and developed into the breeds we have today. Devon Rex cats have a very distinctive wedge-shaped head with enormous ears and a short muzzle, while their Cornish cousins are a little less extreme in appearance. Both breeds can be quite extroverted, vocal, extremely affectionate and people-oriented. They are also active cats whose kitten-like antics last for their lifetime and they can be very inventive in their play.

Not to be confused with . . . the pixies at the end of your garden!

Havana Brown

If you're looking for a cat who knows he's gorgeous and will never let you forget it, think about this breed. One of the most elegant and graceful cats around, the Havana Brown is really just a solid brown coloured Siamese. Like Siamese cats, they can be quite demanding and attention-seeking, and are excellent climbers and door-openers. One to avoid if you have a collection of priceless porcelain on the living room dresser then!

This is a highly intelligent breed of cat that easily learns its name and the word "No"! They make wonderful companion animals whether you plan to show or simply as a very best friend in your home. It is not unusual for a Havana Brown to touch you with a paw to get your attention or to run, then flop on the floor right in your path for a tummy rub.

Not to be confused with . . . a Havana cigar - they're both sleek and brown, but that's where the similarity ends!

Maine Coon

This is the Collie-dog of the cat world – a hard-working cat which has its origins on the farms of New England where it was a popular house cat and ruthless mouse hunter. Just as the Collie is the ultimate farm dog, the Maine Coon is the crème de la crème of farm cats – with just a touch of aristocracy thrown in for good measure!

Nowadays this breed is more commonly seen in the show ring rather than the farmhouse, but wherever he is, he'll always be a hunter at heart, happiest roaming the countryside and terrorising the local mouse population.

Not to be confused with . . . a good old tabby moggy – they may look a little similar from a distance, but close up you can spot the blue blood running through his royal veins!

Manx

What do you call a cat with no tail? A Manx, of course. These little cats, which originate from the Isle of Man in the Irish Sea, are the only breed to be born without a tail (due to a very rare genetic mutation). They also have the distinction of having the shortest body of all domestic pedigree cats – a characteristic that, combined with their lack of tail, tends to mean that these cats are not the best climbers in the world. So if you're after a cat that leaps about the house and chases birds out of the trees, think again. However if you want a friendly, gentle cat and you're not really a tail person, this could be the breed for you!

Did you know . . . people used to believe that Manx cats lost their tails because they were late for Noah's Ark and Noah shut their tail in the door?!

Siamese

This ancient breed is perhaps the oldest of all our cats. They are shorthaired oriental cats with a very distinctive look - a long, elegant nose and mouth, and a sleek, shorthaired body. But apart from their graceful looks, probably the one most obvious characteristic of this breed is their voice. The Siamese voice is legendary and you can hear it from about a mile away! And as well as being the loudest breed of cat, Siamese cats are also one of the most demanding and inquisitive. They are the quintessential "people" cat, and they love to be in your lap, on your bed, at your table and in your heart! As a result, I'd only consider one if you don't mind being bossed around by your cat!

Not to be confused with . . . a meowing foghorn!

Joe's One Top Breed to Avoid . . .

Persian

I know lots of Persian owners will read this and cry in horror, but I couldn't finish this section on breeds without mentioning the reasons why I think this breed should be avoided. My main problem with Persians is that they have been bred for a look which is not compatible with good health. Their squashed faces mean they suffer from a lot of eye and nose problems, as well as breathing difficulties and deformities of their teeth.

To be fair to Persian breeders, there is a movement away from the most extreme types of this breed, and perhaps in time they will manage to breed a truly healthy Persian. Until then, my tip would be to look elsewhere for your cat. If your heart is well and truly set on owning one, then try to find a breeder whose kittens have 'normal' looking faces, rather than looking as if they've run into the back of a bus!

Did you know . . .

That virtually all ginger cats are male, and all tortoiseshell cats are female? It's due to the genes for these colours being linked to the sex chromosomes, so, on the whole, only male cats can have the ginger gene, and only female cats can have the tortie gene. It is possible to the get the occasional 'ginger queen' but the odds are firmly stacked in favour of the good old ginger tom!

3. Tabby Teenagers!

With your new cat settling in at home, there's plenty to do over the next few months to make sure she grows up into a happy and healthy adult cat. Here are my top tips for looking after your cat as she grows from a kitten into a full-sized puss!

Make yourself at home . . .

Most cats are pretty good at making themselves thoroughly at home, and as you let them out of the cat basket will head straight off to the comfiest looking armchair or softest duvet in the house. However, should you not want to share your bed with the cat, or take objection to him curling up in your favourite armchair, here are a few good tips for offering your new cat a comfy alternative.

- *Radiator hammocks* – these furry beds which hang off radiators are a great invention and most cats love them.

- *Vet's beds are the best!* – Ask your vet to supply you with a section of veterinary bedding as it is really comfy, very tough and washable.

- *The airing cupboard – cat heaven!* Pop a cat bed on a shelf in your airing cupboard and you will have one happy pussycat (and lots of hairy towels!).

A wee problem . . .

One of the first things you will want to sort out with your new cat is toilet training. There are few things worse than the smell of stale cat pee, so it's really important to make sure you get your cat litter trained from day one.

The good news is that cats are naturally clean animals, and given the choice will always go to the toilet somewhere where they can bury the waste – such as soil or sand. So toilet training is usually no more complicated than making sure there is a clean litter tray available at all times within easy reach. To begin with you might need to pick up the kitten as soon as he is showing any signs of going to the toilet, and place him in the tray, but he will quickly get the idea and shouldn't need help for more than a day or two.

Top litter tip

Buy cat litter made from recycled newspaper or wood pulp. It's just as efficient as the traditional stuff, and it's much better for the environment.

Another top litter tip!

Never put the litter tray near the food area as cats hate mixing eating and weeing (don't we all!). If both are in the kitchen, try to put them as far away from each other as you can.

Just one final top litter tip!

It's really important to make sure the litter is always fresh, especially when you are first starting to litter train a cat. Cats don't like using a dirty tray, and if they get into the habit of ignoring the litter and going elsewhere you'll soon regret not cleaning the tray out after every visit!

A house kitten is a safe kitten

Until your kitten has been fully vaccinated I would advise you to keep her inside. There's plenty to keep her occupied and entertained, so don't worry about being cruel by keeping her in. The danger with going out is that she might meet other cats, and they could be carrying nasty diseases such as feline leukaemia, and she won't be protected against these infections until a week after her vaccination course has finished.

A trip to the vet

Don't feel that you have to rush your new kitten down to the vet straightaway – let him settle in for a week or so first before you take him in for his first check up and vaccinations. If you've not been to a vet before, ask animal- owning friends for their recommendation, and visit a few practices to find the one with which you feel most comfortable.

Once you've decided on a practice, book an appointment and head down for a full check over. The vet will examine your kitten and (hopefully) give him a clean bill of health before starting his vaccinations and also advising on worming, flea treatment and microchipping – more of which to come.

Vaccines are vital

If there's one tip in this book that you really need to take note of, it's this one! Vaccinations are vital to protect your cat against three really dangerous diseases – cat flu, feline infectious enteritis and feline leukaemia. All that's involved are two injections three or four weeks apart, with the second injection taking place when the cat is around 12 weeks old, followed by annual boosters to keep the immunity up-to-date.

You might find that your kitten is a little sleepy for 24 hours after the injections, but that should be the only side effect you notice.

Did you know?

That the feline leukaemia virus is the second biggest killer of young male cats (after road traffic accidents). A very good reason to protect your cat with regular vaccinations!

Breeders beware

One more tip on the subject of vaccination – if you have
lots of cats because you breed them or house them in
a cattery, there's another disease to vaccinate your cats
against. It's called Chlamydia and it causes all sorts of
problems, including really nasty conjunctivitis. It thrives in
places where there are a lot of cats, and can go through
a household with devastating results – so ask your vet to
add it to the vaccine schedule for your cats if you have
more than five or six in the house.

Worm your way out of trouble!

After vaccination, the next most important thing to think
about is worming. There are a lot of different types of
worms that can live inside your cat's intestines – some are
long and thin (roundworms), some are flat and segmented
(tapeworms), but they all have one thing in common
– they're horrible and you don't want them in your cat!

To make sure your cat is a
worm-free zone, your vet
will recommend dosing him
with a good-quality wormer
every few weeks up to twelve
weeks of age – and then
every three to four months
after that. For more tips
on how to give your cat a
worming tablet, have a look
in the next section.

The dreaded 'F' word!

There are a few unpleasant 'F' words that you might use when your kitten is destroying the curtains or leaving little presents in the flowerpots, but the one I'm thinking of here is 'F' for fleas of course! I've got lots of great tips for sorting out fleas in the next section, but it is really important to start thinking about flea control from an early age, so here are a couple of flea tips for kittens and tabby teenagers . . .

- Make sure your vet checks your kitten for fleas at his first vaccination.

- Check that any flea products you use on young kittens are suitable for use under 12 weeks, as many products can only be safely used on older cats.

- Get on top of any flea infestations in young cats very quickly, as in really severe cases kittens can die because they lose so much blood (fleas live on blood that they suck from the skin).

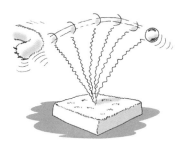

DNA – the ultimate identification

Not satisfied with just a microchip? Well if you want the ultimate in cat protection you could consider signing up to a new service with a company called The Missing Pets Bureau. They take a DNA swab from your cat's mouth and this can be used to prove the identity of your cat in a court of law. The bureau will also hunt down your cat if it goes missing, so if you've got a very valuable (or just particularly adorable) cat, it's well worth considering. Have a look at their website at www.missingpetsbureau.com or call them on 08701 999 000.

The big snip!

Unless you're planning on breeding from your cat, it's vital to get him or her neutered. Un-neutered cats are responsible for countless unwanted stray kittens every year, as well as being at a much higher risk of picking up nasty infections, getting into cat fights and disappearing. It's really not a big deal, just a quick operation at your vet. Most cats recover very quickly and are back to normal within a few days. The best time for the operation is when your kitten is about six months old, although cats as young as three months can be neutered, as can older cats.

A chip in the neck saves lives

If your cat is going to be an outdoor cat it's vital he is permanently identified with a microchip. These tiny little chips – about the size of a grain of rice – are implanted by your vet under the skin of the scruff of his neck, and can be read by a special electronic scanner. They contain a unique number which is registered with your details, so your cat is always identifiable as belonging to you. All vets and rescue centres have these scanners, so if your cat were ever to get lost, or injured, he would be quickly identified and reunited with you.

Don't look!

Just a quick thought for when you are getting your cat microchipped – don't look! The chip is implanted with a really big needle and if you're not keen on injections it could make you feel a bit queasy! (But don't worry about the cat, the needle is so sharp, and their scruff so tough, they rarely feel anything.)

Joe's Kitten Care Diary

Confused by all the things you need to remember with your new kitten? Well don't worry, because here's my easy-to-follow diary to show you what you should be doing and when for the first six months!

7-8 weeks old – bring your kitten home and help her settle in with a comfy bed, clean litter tray, and fresh kitten food.

9 weeks old – your kitten should be settling in at home so it's time for his first trip to the vet for a check over, vaccinations, worming and flea check.

12 weeks old – second vaccinations, repeat worming, and start on routine preventative flea treatment. Also the best time for microchipping and organising pet insurance.

13 weeks old – he's now fully protected by his vaccinations so he can start to go out into the garden.

16 weeks old – repeat worming, and then every 3-4 months.

17 – 20 weeks old – repeat flea treatment (exact frequency depends on the product being used, but generally once every 4 – 5 weeks).

6 months old – neutering.

4. Nose to Tail Health

Keeping your pet in top condition

Looking after a cat is a lifetime's work, and there's always plenty to think about and do in order to keep her in tip-top condition, whatever her age. From fleas to fur balls, here are my top tips for keeping your cat in the very best of health throughout her life!

Fleas!

You sit down in the armchair with your beloved cat and smile as she relaxes into a deep sleep on your lap.

'Ah, how cute,' you think, as you run your hand gently down her back.

Then suddenly you notice something move – a tiny brown speck scurrying through the fur, and you realise that your beloved cat, which you've been cuddling and stroking, is absolutely crawling with FLEAS!

Not a nice moment, seeing a flea on your cat. It somehow leaves you with an uncontrollable desire to itch and scratch for the next day or two! But there are lots of things you can do to make sure that you are never faced with that horrible moment. Here are my top 'flea free' tips for you and your cat…

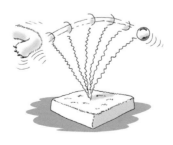

A groom a day keeps the fleas at bay!

Brush your cat once a day and you'll spot the first signs of a flea infestation straight away. Concentrate on his back, just in front of the tail, because this is where fleas tend to live. If you check every day then you can take action at the first sign of trouble.

Is it fluff? Is it dirt? No, it's a flea!

Here's how you can tell if the tiny specks you've found in the fur of your cat are fleas, or just bits of muck. Just ask yourself the following three questions and you'll soon have a diagnosis!

1. Is it oval and about 2-3mm long?
2. Is it moving?
3. Is it brown?

If you've can answer yes to all of the questions, I'm afraid you've just seen a flea! If not, I think you've found a bit of dandruff or muck, and you can breathe a huge sigh of relief!

Flea detective!

You won't always see a live flea if your cat has an infestation, as they only hang around long enough to feed and lay eggs. So therefore, just because you haven't seen a flea, doesn't necessarily mean that your cat hasn't got a flea problem – but there is a way in which you can turn detective and find the tell-tale evidence you need to make a firm diagnosis. What you need to do is comb through you cat's fur along his back, and collect on a sheet of white paper any tiny black specks that come out. Then dab them with some damp cotton wool. If the specks are flea dirt (the waste fleas pass after feeding), they'll stain the paper red-brown because they contain traces of blood. This is all the evidence you need to convict Mr Flea and start treatment!

Vet treatments are best

Now I'm not just saying this because I'm a vet – it really is true that many of the so-called flea drops and sprays you can get from the pet shop are no use at all, and the only really effective ones have to be prescribed by vets. The best and most convenient treatments are the drops that you put on the back of the neck. Cats hate being sprayed, so these drops tend to be much easier to use, and they are really effective.

Eggs-terminate the problem!

Dealing with the fleas on your cat is only half the problem. The other half of the problem is in your carpets and it's the thousands of eggs and larvae that each flea produces during their lives. The eggs drop off your cat and end up in the carpet, where they develop into larvae and then adult fleas – and unless you sort out these developing fleas, you'll find it hard to get rid of the problem completely.

To kill off all these eggs and larvae, you'll need to buy a can of powerful household spray (again from your vet). Here are a couple of tips to make sure you sort the problem out 100%:

- Vacuum thoroughly and wash all the cat's bedding before you spray, as this will get rid of a lot of the eggs and larvae.

- Spray everywhere in the house that the cat goes – living room, kitchen, bedrooms, and even the bathroom and airing cupboard if necessary.

- Before you spray put out the cat and shut the cat flap (or take him out of the house in a box if he doesn't usually go out), and keep all the family out of the house as well for a couple of hours

Worms!

If there's one thing worse than the thought of a flea crawling around on the skin of your cat, it's the thought of a worm wriggling around inside her! Cats can pick up tapeworms and roundworms from all sorts of places, and they can cause a range of health problems including a poor coat, diarrhoea, weight loss and anaemia.

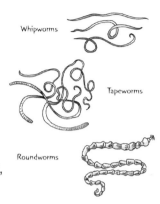

Whipworms

Tapeworms

Roundworms

That's the bad news – the good news is that dealing with worms is pretty easy. Just follow these top tips and your cat should never have a wormy problem!

Worm your cat three or four times a year

Unlike flea treatments, worming tablets and powders don't protect against worms for any length of time - they just kill the worms that are in the intestine when the treatment is given. So to keep your cat free of worms you need to repeat the treatment on a regular basis. For cats that spend most of their lives indoors, two or three times a year is fine, but for cats that go out a lot, you need to worm them at least every three months.

The mouse's revenge!

Next time you pity that poor little mouse your cat has just dragged into the kitchen, remember that it could be the mouse, not the cat, which has the last laugh. That's because eating small mammals like mice is the main way in which cats pick up worms. So while your cat might have won the battle with the mouse, the worms the mouse delivers could mean that he wins the war!

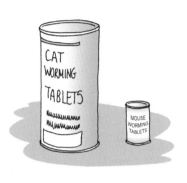

(The tip here is that if your cat grows up to be a hunter, you should worm him more regularly than if he is a house cat.)

Menu of the day – worming tablets, powders or paste?

As the old saying (nearly) goes 'there's more than one way to worm a cat' and this is very true. Most vets will prescribe tablets, but there are also worming powders, granules, pastes and injections. And even if you do opt for tablets, there are still choices to make – a little tablet that you can pop down your cat's mouth or hide in his food, or a big tasty tablet that he'll eat from your hand? Let your vet guide you – and work out what type of wormer suits your cat best. Some will be no problem to give tablets to, whereas others will be much easier to dose with granules in the food or an injection at the vet.

How to worm a cat – without losing a finger!

Recommending that you worm your cat regularly is the easy bit – but what about actually giving the tablet? It almost seems as if all cats have been taught 101 ways to avoid swallowing a worming tablet by their mothers when they were little kittens – they scratch, twist, wriggle, bite, and then spit out the tablet before disappearing up the curtains and staring back at the ruins of your living room with a triumphant meow!

Well, there is a way to give cats worming tablets (and any other tablet they need), which most vets use, and which works in 99% of cases. Of course there are always one or two cats who are absolute masters of the art of refusing tablets, but for the majority of cats, this technique is pretty much foolproof.

To do this you need a willing (and brave!) accomplice, a sturdy table, the worming tablet – and, of course, the cat. Sit the cat on the table and ask your helper to hold him firmly around the chest and front legs. In this position the cat is well restrained and can't use his front claws to scratch you.

(continued......!)

Next, you should take the worming tablet and approach the cat from the front. Reach you left hand behind his head and hold his head firmly by the cheeks, then tilt the head backwards until his throat is straight and he is looking up at the ceiling. Then comes the tricky part! With your right index finger, pull his mouth open and drop the tablet down into his throat.

The key is to drop the tablet so it lands right at the base of his tongue. Then, before he has time to react, give the tablet a quick poke with your finger so he swallows, and whip your finger back out and close his mouth firmly, holding it shut for a few moments until you're sure the tablet has gone down.

Then finally, assuming you still have your fingers, release the cat, sit down with a strong drink, and allow yourself a smug, triumphant smile as the defeated cat slinks out of the cat flap!

It's never too soon to start grooming

It really pays to get your cat used to being brushed at an early age, so he doesn't object when he's older (and his teeth and claws are sharper!). Get your kitten used to being brushed by playing with him with the brush, and giving him little treats. Gradually start to run the brush through his fur, but keep it fun and enjoyable, and don't persist if he decides he's had enough. Over a few weeks he should get accustomed to being groomed – and you shouldn't have any more problems in the future.

Great balls of fur!

Fur balls are a common problem for a lot of cats. They are literally great big balls of fur which form a solid, matted lump in the stomach, and they happen because when cats groom themselves they swallow lots of fur. Most of the time these fur balls will pass out of the stomach and end up in the faeces, but sometimes they get too big and the cat has to retch them up. This can be a bit unpleasant (especially if you're having dinner at the time!) but it's not a cause for worry unless it becomes a persistent problem. If your cat is constantly retching then she probably has got a fur ball stuck, and it's time to take some action.

Grooming makes your cat one of the family

It's a really good idea to get into the habit of grooming your cat on a regular basis. Not only does it keep her coat in great condition, and helps you spot any skin problems or fleas straight away, it also helps form a bond between you and your cat. In the wild, mutual grooming is a vital part of social bonding, and by taking part in this activity with your cat, you'll help to make her feel part of your family.

The longer the hair, the more frequent the grooming

Shorthaired cats don't really suffer if they're not groomed very often, but longhaired cats really need daily brushing to prevent tangles and knots forming in their fur. Use a 'slicker' brush to remove the dead hair and tangles from his coat and then a soft brush to finish him off.

Cod liver oil paste shifts fur balls

The best way to sort out a cat with a fur ball is to buy a tube of special cod liver oil paste from your pet shop or vet. This helps the fur ball slip through the intestines and out the other end! Simply wipe an inch or so of the paste on your cat's paw and he'll lick it off and swallow it. Within a couple of days the offending fur-ball should have been passed, and you can enjoy your dinner without the accompanying sound of a retching cat!

Claws 'n paws

Keeping your cat's claws well trimmed is a good idea if you don't want him to ruin your best sofa or scratch your arm when he climbs onto your lap. The best, and easiest way, to keep his claws short is to provide him with a scratch post, which you can buy from a pet shop. Alternatively, if you don't mind a bit of DIY and you want to save a few quid, get yourself a couple of pieces of sturdy timber and cover them with old carpet off cuts. This will make a perfectly good scratching post and should keep him away from your furniture!

Did you know...?

That cats scratch for two reasons. One is to keep their claws in good condition by removing the top layers of keratin. The other reason is territorial – cats leave scratches as a kind of feline graffiti to mark their territory, and the process of scratching also leaves their scent behind which helps to let other cats know who's the boss of the area!

Ear's a good tip!

If your cat has got waxy, smelly ears, it's almost certainly caused by tiny little mites (called otodectes cynotis). These parasites cause intense irritation and can lead to nasty bacterial ear infections, which will require your vet's attention. If your cat has just got a mild case – some black ear wax and head shaking – try cleaning out the wax with some ear cleaner solution, and use one of the veterinary flea drops (applied in the normal way, to the back of the neck – not down the ear!) which will also kill off ear mites (ask your vet for details).

The cat's whiskers

Did you know that cats use their whiskers to judge whether they can fit through small spaces – so don't ever trim your cat's whiskers otherwise he'll end up getting stuck in a gap in the fence!

Wear sunscreen!

You might not think that cats are at much risk of skin cancer from too much sun - after all, they're mainly covered in protective fur. Well, while it's true that their fluffy coats protect most of their bodies, there are a couple of places where the sun can get through and sunburn, even cancer, is not that rare in some cats.

Most at risk are their ear tips, and it's white cats that suffer most problems, just as fair-skinned people are more at risk of sunburn than darker people. If you have a cat with white ears, use sunscreen regularly through the summer to protect them. It's best to use a cream designed for children, as this is less likely to irritate their skin, and make sure it's factor 40 or higher. Apply the cream two or three times a day during hot sunny spells, and your cat should be able to enjoy the sunshine without risking burns or skin cancer.

Stay in control!

All these health care tips are all very well if you have a nice, friendly cat. But what if your puss is more wild tiger than tame tabby? Here are a couple of top tips to help you handle your cat if things aren't going to plan!

Clothes pegs can help tame a tabby tantrum!

'How?' I hear you ask – well it's pretty easy really. Just pop a clothes peg on the back of your cat's neck and you should find that she settles down brilliantly. The reason this trick works is that it simulates the way cats' mothers hold them with their teeth when they're kittens. Pinching this area with the peg reassures the cat and makes her feel like her mother is telling her to behave well!

74

Scruff treatment

If a clothes peg isn't doing the trick for you, try holding your troublesome cat by his scruff. Grasp as much of the loose skin at the back of his neck as you can and hold tight. You won't do him any harm or hurt him, but with a good grip here, he shouldn't be able to get you with teeth or claws.

Throw in the towel!

This is the real last resort – for the manic moggy who is lashing out and climbing the walls – and it's a technique favoured by vets worldwide when the softly-softly approach hasn't worked. All it involves is wrapping the cat up in an old towel. Make sure you get all of those legs tightly held inside the towel – although this can be easier said than done, as angry cats seem to have at least ten legs when you're trying to get them wrapped up!

5. Cats Behaving Badly

When people think of badly behaved pets, they probably picture a destructive or aggressive dog. But in fact, behavioural problems are just as common in cats, and some of the more serious ones such as aggression and urine marking can make life a real misery for owner and cat alike. The key to preventing and treating these problems in cats is to understand their way of thinking – get inside the head of your cat, and you should be able to sort out even the most serious behavioural issues.

It's all about territory

If there's one tip for understanding a cat's behaviour it's this – never forget that cats are territorial animals. This fact is at the heart of all feline behaviour, from aggression to messing in the house, and it's the main behavioural difference between cats and dogs. Whereas dogs are pack animals, cats are lone hunters by nature, and looking after their territory is often the single most important thing in their lives. If they don't feel secure in this area of their lives, everything else can fall apart – often with disastrous results!

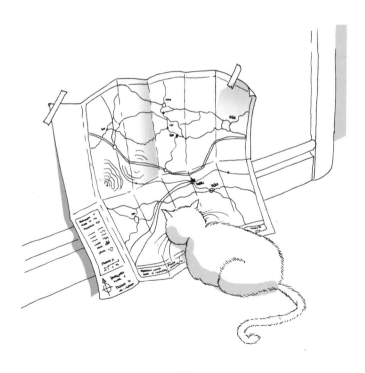

It's as easy as 1-2-3 . . .

A cat's territory is not just an area where they hunt. It is made up of three distinct zones, and understanding the different purposes of these zones can really help you sort out your badly behaved cat.

Zone 1 is the most important. This is the inner zone where they should be able to totally relax and feel safe from any threat. In most domestic cats, Zone 1 is your house, and strange cats intruding into this area will cause immense stress to your cat – with the likely consequence of serious behavioural problems.

Zone 2 is your cat's primary hunting zone, and is often made up of your garden. In this area cats will do their best to chase off intruders, and persistent rivals can cause stress and behavioural problems.

And finally, Zone 3. This is the much wider area that your cat will wander through when he's out on a hunting mission at night. Here he's happy to meet and greet other cats, as long as they respect his scent marks and don't try and muscle in on his patch!

How to spot a happy cat!

The other important thing to learn that will help you get to grips with a badly behaved cat is how to spot her moods. Get this right and you will know when she's happy to be stroked and fussed – and more importantly, when it's best to stay well clear until she's feeling better!

Ears upright, eyes wide open, whiskers relaxed . . . a happy, relaxed cat – it's safe to stroke her and tickle that fluffy tummy!

Ears back, whiskers slightly forward, pupils wide open . . . she's anxious and stressed. Time to give her some space.

Ears flat, whiskers forward, pupils wide open and eyes narrowed . . . watch out, she's getting angry! Best not to touch her, or she could lash out in this mood!

Don't be dominated

There's nothing quite like rubbing your cat's lovely tabby tummy, as she purrs contentedly on your lap. Everything is peaceful and relaxed…

…until she suddenly switches from passive puss to terrible tabby and lashes out at your hand with her claws and sinks her teeth into your arm!

'What did I do wrong?' you ask yourself, 'Was it me? Did I hurt her?'

Don't worry. It wasn't you – it was her. Some cats like to be dominant, and every now and then will decide to show you who's boss by switching to aggressive mode. The best way to prevent this behaviour is to look out for the warning signs – a slowly wagging tail and narrowing eyes – and immediately stop stroking her. Then leave her alone for a few minutes before starting to give her attention again.

It wasn't me!

Apart from the dominant cat who lashes out to prove she's the top cat, the other common cause of cat-person aggression is the cat who is wound up and tense because they can't get at another cat which is 'trespassing' on his patch. The tip here is 'beware the growling cat on the windowsill'! If you go up to him in this mood, he's likely to take his frustration out on you, even though his beef is with the cat and not you – you just happen to be the nearest victim he can get his claws into!

It's cat-eat-cat in here!

There's nothing worse than two cats going at each other hammer and tongs – and especially if it's in your home, and it's your two beloved cats involved! But unfortunately this kind of cat vs. cat aggression is quite a common problem – and can be really tricky to sort out.

In serious cases, where the cats are at each other every time they meet, there's little option but to separate them for a while. Feed them in separate rooms for a week or two, but swap the rooms around every day so they don't forget each other's scent. Then gradually bring them together, using cat boxes if required, and feed them in opposite corners of the same room. Over a few weeks, bring their feeding areas closer together, until they will tolerate eating next to each other.

Five ways to cure a cat that pees in the house

This is one of the most common behavioural problems in domestic cats, and the cause is often territorial. Cats that are stressed because another cat is invading Zone 2, or even worse, Zone 1 of their territory, will be desperate to reinforce the scent marking in this area – and the best way to do this is to urine mark. Sorting out the problem can be tricky, but try these top tips and you should be able to keep your house smelling sweet!

1. Fit a magnetic cat flap which will allow only your cats into the house. This will keep unwanted intruders out, and reduce your cat's urge to urine mark as a result.

2. Cat-proof the garden by putting high fences and spiky plants around the perimeter. This should reduce the number of feline trespassers in Zone 2 of your cat's territory.

3. Arm yourself with a water pistol and scare off any unknown cats that come into the garden or house.

4. Wipe a tea-towel on your cat's paws and then rub this onto the area where he is peeing. His feet have tiny scent glands, and by wiping this around the house, you're helping him reinforce his territory without resorting to peeing.

5. Use a pheromone diffuser. These plug-in devices from your vet release a calming cat pheromone which will help to relax your cat and stop the urine marking.

That's my best top!

Cats can be strange animals, there's no denying it. And there are few stranger cats than the ones with a penchant for eating clothes! No-one really knows why some cats like eating fabric, but some people think it might be due to early weaning or stress, and it seems to be Siamese cats that are most likely to have this weird habit.

Fabric-eating cats will suck and chew at all sorts of things – from socks to slippers – and the consequences can be more serious than just damage to your favourite outfits. In some cases, some cats will actually swallow bits of cloth, and this can get stuck inside and require a major operation.

So what can you do if your cat takes a fancy to the contents of your wardrobe? Well, the easiest solution is to stop the cat from getting access to clothes – so shut him out of the bedroom for example. You can also give him an alternative to chewing on clothes by offering him bones or rawhide chews, and in an extreme cases, you can even sprinkle a little chilli powder on the items you want him to stop chewing!

Taming a terrible tabby

A last little tip on the subject of behaviour – if you want to tame a stray or wild cat, try feeding him cat biscuits from your hand. Once he's happy taking the food from you, try giving him a gentle stroke at the same time. Keep this up and he'll soon get used to you and become a real pussycat!

6. Meals for Moggies

If there's one thing you really have to get right when owning a cat, that's feeding. As the old saying goes 'you are what you eat' and this is just as relevant to your cat as it is to you. Get your cat's diet wrong and he'll run the risk of all sorts of health problems, from diabetes to bone disease. But get it spot on, and you'll have a fit, healthy and very contented cat on your hands!

Cats are carnivores

This is the big number one rule when it comes to feeding domestic cats. Unlike dogs and lots of other animals, cats are what are known as 'obligate carnivores'. In plain English this means that they have to eat meat in order to survive. The reason for this is that cats can't make one of the really vital amino acids (the building blocks of protein) called taurine, and they rely on animal protein for this nutrient. Without meat, cats quickly lose condition and decline – and eventually die from malnutrition, so it's absolutely vital to keep your cat on a meaty diet.

Some mice are nice!

Whatever you feed you cat, the occasional mouse or vole will help to add a little variety to her feeding, and make 100% sure she's getting a really balanced diet. Now I'm not suggesting you actually feed her mice of course – just advising that you turn a blind eye when you see her chasing a poor little mouse around the kitchen and let her get on with her natural business. If you're a bit squeamish about the whole hunting thing, just remember that what she's eating in her dish is also made of meat and came from an animal, and hunting is not that different really!

Ready meals

Having the occasional mouse is one thing, but modern domestic cats can't be expected to survive just on hunting – most don't have the opportunity and few would have the skills to make a true living out of mousing. So nearly all modern cats live on ready-prepared processed foods from tins or bags. These diets first appeared about 70 years ago, and quickly replaced the mix of table scraps and mice that most house cats would have eaten before their introduction.

These convenience diets are great for owners and can be good for cats too – but there are drawbacks and things to watch out for. Here are my top ten useful facts about commercial cat foods:

1. Tinned cat foods are 80% water – which is about the same as fresh meat – and don't usually contain preservatives.

2. Dried cat foods are only 10% water, but often have preservatives to keep them fresh.

3. Dried foods are more hygienic and better for your cat's teeth.

4. All complete cat foods must contain the minimum requirements of all the essential nutrients a cat needs to stay healthy.

5. You can feed cat food to dogs (although it is a bit too rich for them) but not dog food to cats as it doesn't have enough protein in it.

6. Cheap cat foods will contain less real meat protein and more 'textured vegetable protein' which is much less good for your cat.

7. All the ingredients will be listed on the packet or tin and it's well worth reading this small print to see what's really in the food you're serving to your cat.

8. Watch out for labels that say 'chicken flavour' or 'with beef', as this food will only contain a tiny amount of the real meat and the rest will be animal by-products and vegetable protein.

9. Cheap cat foods will contain mainly animal by-products like feathers, feet and other bits you really don't want your cat to eat!

10. You get what you pay for – premium cat foods will contain much more real meat and much less rubbish!

Variety is the spice of your cat's life!

While leaving a dish of dried biscuits down all day for your cat might work well and give him all the nutrients and energy he needs, it can get a little dull day after day. So my tip is to do what most cat owners find works really well, and feed a small meal of 'wet' food once a day to add a little variety to his diet. This wet food can be from a tin or pouch, or it can be something more interesting such as some home-cooked fish or chicken, or even fresh liver if you're feeling particularly generous! Take a look at some of the tips coming up if you are thinking about doing a little home cooking for your cat.

How to avoid a messy accident . . .

Just a quick tip – always feed your cat in the same place rather than move his dish around the kitchen. This way you won't forget where you've put the dish and accidentally put your foot in it! Treading in cat food not only messes up your cat's dinner, it also can ruin your socks as cat food is notorious for leaving rather unpleasant smells and stains on clothing!

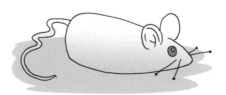

How much to feed?

Every cat is an individual so it's impossible to say exactly how much food your cat will need to eat each day. A lively, energetic young cat who spends his time racing around the garden stalking birds will need lots more energy than an elderly cat who spends most of his time by the fire for example – and pregnant queens and growing kittens will also need much more food than the average cat. Overall though, a normal cat who lives a fairly normal life will need to consume somewhere around 300 kilocalories every day – roughly a tenth of what a person needs.

Let the cat decide!

Cats are much more sensible eaters than dogs who, given half a chance, only stop eating when they are so full they can't move. In the wild, cats would eat little meals every few hours (one mouse at a time!), rather than gorging on a big feast once a day. So the best way to feed your domestic cat healthily is to let him graze on a dish of dried food throughout the day. He'll eat when he wants to and most cats are not so greedy that they overeat.

Joe's top five recipes for home-cooked cat food

If you want to put a bit of variety and healthy home-cooked goodness into your cat's diet, there's nothing better than preparing a fresh meal for him once a week or so. Work you way through these recipes to find out which ones he prefers – and if you fancy improvising to come up with some new ideas, check out my next tips which will give you all the dos and don'ts.

1. Chicken in a creamy vegetable sauce – simply oven cook or steam a small breast of chicken, and pour over a small amount of sauce made by blending together a couple of little pieces of carrot and broccoli or a few peas, and mixing in a couple of tablespoons of cream (use yoghurt if your cat is overweight).

2. Fish and brown rice – take a small fillet of oily fish and steam it until well-cooked (raw fish is not good for cats), add some cooked brown rice and mash together. You can add a little amount of mayonnaise too but not all cats will like this as much as we do!

3. Liver and mince – fry up some diced liver with some fresh beef mince using a small amount of oil. Cook the liver for longer than the mince as this helps reduce the excessive vitamin A which can cause problems in raw or undercooked liver. The mince can be as rare as your cat likes!

4. Steak à la egg shell – this might sound strange but ground up egg shell is a great way of adding the essential calcium which is lacking in most meats. Simply grind up an egg shell and sprinkle a generous pinch into a bowl of diced steak pieces, before lightly frying the meat. You can scramble the leftover egg and serve this as a side dish with the meat if you're feeling really generous!

5. Fishy nuggets – these are a great treat which you can store in the fridge for a week or so, and are guaranteed to appeal to even the fussiest cat! Simply combine ½ cup of mackerel (tinned or filleted fresh) with a cup of breadcrumbs, a beaten egg, a tablespoon of vegetable oil, and ½ teaspoon of brewers yeast if you have some. Then drop the mixture in ¼ teaspoonfuls onto a greased baking tray and cook in a hot oven for 8 minutes.

The do's and don'ts of cooking for cats

If you want to feed your cat regular home-prepared meals, here are a few key things to remember:

- **Do** feed a varied diet.

- **Don't** use raw fish or liver more than once a week.

- **Do** add pureed vegetables to your meals.

- **Don't** give milk to your cat if he reacts badly to it – some cats will have diarrhoea when they drink cow's milk.

- **Do** make sure your cat gets plenty of calcium by adding ground up eggshells or bone meal to any meaty dishes he has regularly.

- **Don't** give him leftovers – they are usually very fatty and unhealthy.

- **Do** add brewers yeast to his meals – this supplement is rich in lots of nutrients and great for the skin, coat and immune system.

- **Don't** feed raw eggs – they contain avidin which reduces the availability of one of the B vitamins, and can contain salmonella.

- **Do** ask your vet for advice, especially if you are thinking about feeding your cat solely on home-cooked food.

The green, green grass of home

Some cats love eating grass and it is quite a healthy snack food for them. It sometimes makes them sick if they eat too much, but in general it is fine and you shouldn't discourage your cat from a little gentle grazing. If your cat is an indoor cat, why not see if she'd fancy a little dish of freshly cut grass occasionally?

Cats love rain water!

Ever wondered why you never see your cat drinking from his water bowl in the kitchen? Well the reason is probably that like lots of cats, he really doesn't like the taste of tap water with all the additives that are in it. Instead, he'll be getting his water outside, drinking from puddles and ponds; this water might be murky and muddy, but he prefers this to the chemicals in our water. So if you want to save your cat from having to search out his water supply outside, help him out by giving him a dish of fresh rainwater collected from a water butt in the garden – or if you're feeling really generous, how about a bit of that bottled spring water you drink yourself?

Fat cats!

Obesity is a growing problem (excuse the pun!) for cats worldwide, with some estimates suggesting that six out of ten cats are now officially fat! If your cat is more fat-cat than fit-cat then it's time to do something about it – and the first place to start is by looking at his diet. Here are my top three tips for helping your fat cat shed those extra pounds with a healthy diet:

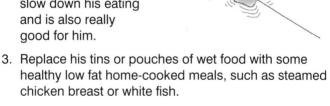

1. Switch his dried food to a 'light' or low calorie version of his normal biscuits – or choose a high quality, low protein brand which is naturally less fattening.

2. Mix his dried food with shredded raw vegetables – this will slow down his eating and is also really good for him.

3. Replace his tins or pouches of wet food with some healthy low fat home-cooked meals, such as steamed chicken breast or white fish.

7. Top Vet Tips

With a bit of luck and plenty of TLC your cat will remain healthy and well throughout her life – but if and when illness does strike, it's important to recognise the symptoms and take the appropriate action. Here are my top vet tips to help you cope with all the common cat health problems:

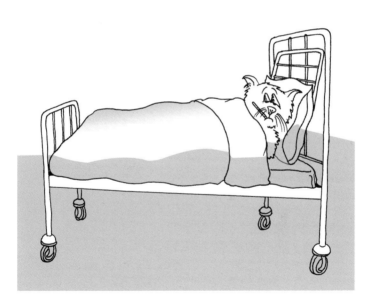

Cat bites

If I had to name the number one cause of ill cats coming into the surgery, it would definitely be 'cat bites'. Thanks to cats' territorial instincts and the high density of cat populations in most towns and cities, conflicts between cats are all too common – and the end result is usually an unpleasant infected bite wound. These injuries can cause serious problems, because cats' mouths are full of nasty bacteria, and these get injected into the flesh when they bite. The resulting infection causes a lot of pain and swelling, and can lead to even more serious problems if the bite is in a tricky area such as the face.

How to tell if your cat is a coward or bully . . .

How much do you know about the character of your cat when he's out of the house? Do you think he's the kind of cat who would start a fight? Or is he a timid puss who'd run away at the first sign of danger?

Well there's one way to get a pretty good idea. If he does end up in a scrap and gets bitten, you can tell a lot about him from the site of the wound. If it's a head wound, he's likely to be the bully who started the fight – but if the wound is on his tail then he was running away when the other cat got him!

Five signs of a cat bite

Not sure if your cat has been bitten? Here are the five most common symptoms to look out for:

1. Limping with a sore leg when you touch it.
2. Obvious swelling on the face, leg or tail.
3. Miserable, off food and generally depressed.
4. Tail hanging down and not moving normally.
5. Nasty smelling ooze from an obvious wound.

Treating a cat bite – the three 'A's

If you suspect that your cat has been bitten, the following three As should sort out the problem:

Antiseptic. Clean the wound with a diluted antiseptic solution such as TCP or Dettol, and then head down to the surgery to see your vet.

Antibiotic. Your vet will prescribe antibiotics to clear up the infection.

Anti-inflammatory. Your vet will inject an anti-inflammatory drug to reduce the swelling and pain of the bite wound.

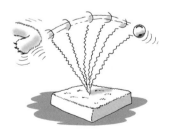

Vomiting

You're sitting down to a lovely candle-lit dinner, when all of a sudden the romantic peace is shattered by a loud retching noise from the corner of the kitchen. You get up and go to see what's going on – is it a sickly burglar? Or a fox stuck in the cat flap? No, you find, it's just the cat. He's hunched miserably over a pile of nasty-looking sick, retching with great spasms of his entire body.

What should you do? Can you ignore the cat and get back to the romantic dinner – or is he in need of an emergency trip to the vet?

Well, my advice is to get back to the romantic dinner. Cats are very good at being sick and some animals will bring up their food on a regular basis because they bolt their food down, or have a fur ball problem. Vomiting can be a sign of more serious problems such as inflammatory bowel disease, gastro-enteritis or kidney disease, but you should only really worry if he is being sick a lot more than normal and is miserable as well.

Assuming he's a well, healthy cat, here's what I would suggest you do to try to sort out a cat that is sick on a regular basis:

- Worm him with a good quality worming tablet from your vet.

- Use a cod liver oil paste to shift any fur balls.

- Make him a special food bowl which slows down his eating – you could try putting his food in a deep, narrow food container.

- Feed him small meals several times a day rather than one or two big meals.

Diarrhoea!

Not a nice problem to have to deal with, but it's important to sort out because, if left untreated, diarrhoea leads to serious complications such as dehydration. This is what you should do:

- Withhold food for 12-24 hours. This might sound cruel but resting the intestine is the best and quickest way to sort out the problem.

- Offer plenty of water.

- Make up a re-hydration solution by mixing a pint of warm water with a teaspoon of salt and a tablespoon of sugar. Offer him this to drink as well as water.

- Cook him some plain white fish or chicken breast after the starving period and feed small amounts three or four times a day for a couple of days.

- Gradually reintroduce his normal food over the next three days.

- Take him straight to the vet if there's no improvement.

Fibre cures constipation!

At the other end of the unpleasant bowel problem spectrum is constipation, which is quite common and can lead to serious internal problems if not sorted out. The best and easiest cure is to add fibre to your cat's diet by mixing a little bran or grated veg such as pumpkin or carrot into his food. Start with a tiny amount and increase it gradually as too much, too fast will cause diarrhoea and wind – not nice for you or him!

You can brush your cat's teeth!

It might sound a bit over the top, but brushing really is the best way to keep your cat's teeth in top condition. Arm yourself with a finger brush (a plastic cover with bristles which slips over your finger – get one from the pet shop or vet) and some special cat toothpaste (which comes in lovely flavours such as 'poultry' and 'tripe'!) and get brushing! Once a day is fine, and the younger you start, the more chance you have of your cat being compliant – and not taking your finger off!

But if you don't fancy brushing . . .

Try a special gel called 'Logic' which you cat get from your vet. You just put it in her food and it helps dissolve tartar as she eats. It's not quite as effective as brushing – but if your cat won't let you near her teeth with your finger brush, it's certainly better than doing nothing.

A trip to the dentist!

With a diet of convenience foods and not a toothbrush in sight, it's not surprising that lots of cats have bad teeth. The symptoms to look out for include bad breath, going off their food or only eating on one side of the mouth, and weight loss. Your vet should check your cat's teeth every year at her annual check up and booster vaccination, and may recommend a dental operation to sort out really bad teeth. But it's far better to prevent her teeth getting to the stage where they need this kind of treatment, so here are my top tips for keeping your cat's gnashers pearly and healthy!

Dried food cleans teeth

This fact might be disputed by some, but in most vets' experience it's easy to spot those cats that don't eat very much dried food because they have much less healthy teeth. Eating crunchy biscuits definitely helps to clean plaque and tartar off the teeth, and your cat should eat at least some dried food every day.

Eczema and acne

It's not just we who can suffer spots and scabs on our skin. Underneath their fur, cats can have all manner of skin problems, ranging from a few spots to full-blown skin infections. The key things to look out for include:

- Over-grooming – a cat that spends much more time than usual licking and grooming.

- Rubbing – cats that are itchy will often rub their backs against chairs and table legs.

- Hair loss – check underneath, in the groin area, as this is where lots of cats tend to lose fur.

- Gritty skin – if your cat feels 'gritty' when you run your hand through his coat, there's definitely a skin problem going on.

There are loads of possible causes of skin diseases, but the three most common ones are fleas, stress and allergies. It's always worth ruling out fleas as a possible cause from day one – so use a good quality flea product from your vet and treat the house as well if necessary. Next, try to identify any new or unusual stresses which could be affecting your cat – such as a new cat getting into the garden, or perhaps a new baby? If you can do something about these stresses, such as keep the invading cat out, then do so, but if not, or if things still aren't improving, you need to head down to the vet. He or she will work out what the most likely cause is, and treat the condition using antibiotics to clear up any infection, and possibly steroids to stop the itching and over-grooming.

Ten reasons to take your cat to the vet

There are certain symptoms that could mean your cat has a serious illness that needs the attention of your vet. If you are worried about any of the following, it's safest to get a thorough check over, as it's always better to be safe than sorry.

1. Drinking and weeing much more than normal – this could indicate that your cat has kidney disease or diabetes.

2. Not eating for two days or more – often a sign that your cat has a high temperature and needs treatment.

3. Limping or not using a leg – could be just a strain or bruise but worth getting your vet to check for fractures or dislocations.

4. Third eyelids across – these are extra eyelids that come across from the corner of the eye when cats are ill or have some eye diseases.

5. Sneezing or coughing.

6. Straining to urinate – an emergency, see in the last section for more details.

7. Bloody diarrhoea or vomit.

8. Marked weight loss – it's always worth keeping a check on your cat's weight so you can tell if weight loss is real or imagined.

9. Laboured breathing.

10. Depression – any cat which becomes suddenly withdrawn, dull and lethargic needs to be checked over.

8. Old Age Pension-purrs!

Just like us, cats change as they get older, and looking after an elderly cat requires a little more dedication and knowledge than when she was younger. The first step is to get an idea of how old your cat is in human terms, so you can relate to her age as if she were a person. Then have a look through the rest of these tips to help you ease your cat through her old age as happily and healthily as possible.

I remember the good old days when I used to chase this stuff!

How old is your cat?

Working out an exact human age for your cat is impossible, but here's a formula which will give you a pretty good idea of roughly how old she would be were she a person:

- The first year counts as 15 years.
- The second year counts as 10 years.
- All subsequent years count as 4 years.
- So a 10-year old cat is $15+10+(4 \times 8) = 57$.
- And a 15-year old cat is $15+10+(4 \times 13) = 77$.

Cats deserve to retire in style!

Once your cat starts to show signs of old age – he's less active than he used to be, a bit thinner and frailer – then it's time to make sure he's as happy and comfy as possible. No more chilly nights on the kitchen floor or fighting with the younger cats for his share of food; it's time he got a little special VIP treatment to ease his old body. So why not buy him a top-of-the-range cat bed and place it next to the warmest radiator for him, and give him his own feeding area away from any other pets. And don't forget to pamper him that little bit more than you used to, with a few extra fresh meals and healthy treats.

Ease those old bones!

Just like older people, arthritis is very common in elderly cats, and can cause a lot of pain and discomfort. The main signs are a reluctance to jump up or run as much as he used to, especially in cold and wet weather, and changes in his personality such as increased aggression (caused by the pain and discomfort). Your vet can help by prescribing anti-inflammatory drugs and supplements such as glucosamine and chondritin, but there are also some things you can do at home to help ease the pain of his arthritic joints:

- A covered hot water bottle or special heated pad in his bed will help keep his joints warm and reduce the pain and swelling he feels.

- Encourage regular short periods of exercise such as a trot around the garden or gentle play indoors to help keep him mobile.

- If he is overweight, ease the strain on his joints by reducing his weight with a low calorie diet.

Raise his game!

A quick tip if your older cat is tending to be sick more frequently – raise his bowl up off the ground by putting it on a couple of old telephone directories. This reduces the acid reflux from his stomach and will make him more comfortable when he eats.

Keep an old boy looking good!

As your cat gets older you'll probably find that his coat starts to get a little less glossy and more prone to tangles and mats. This is because older cats are less flexible than they used to be, and find it harder to groom themselves as thoroughly as they need to. So help him out with regular grooming sessions to keep his coat in top condition. This also gives you the chance to give him a thorough daily check, so you'll spot any new lumps or bumps straightaway.

Treat her to a pedicure!

As well as knotted coats, older cats tend to suffer from overgrown claws, which can even grow right round and into the pad if not checked and trimmed regularly. As they get older and less active, their claws tend to be worn down less than when they were climbing trees and chasing mice in their younger days. It's best to get your vet to check her nails every few months, and trim them if required, but you can do them yourself. All you need is a pair of good nail trimmers from a pet shop or vet – choose the ones with curved blades which encircle the nail. Then, with a trusted assistant holding the cat, simply trim the nails back until they are level with the bottom of her pads. If you can see the pink quick, make sure you leave at least 2-3mm beyond this when you make your cut.

Warm, smelly food is great for older cats!

As cats get older they often lose their sense of smell a little – and since their appetite is largely driven by smell, this can mean they eat less, and lose weight as a result. So try gently warming up your cat's wet food in the microwave (make sure it's only warm and not hot!) and add in some really smelly things such as tinned pilchards.

Blood tests

As your cat advances in years, it's vital to pick up on any health problems as soon as possible. All too often, by the time symptoms become obvious, it's too late to do much about the problem, so spotting the earliest stages of disease is vital – which is where regular blood tests come in. Nowadays all vets' surgeries will be able to offer detailed blood tests for older cats, which will pick up the very earliest signs of diseases such as kidney failure. Making an early diagnosis means you and your vet can start your cat on treatment which could prolong his life. If your cat's getting on in years, then book him in for a thorough MOT and blood test in the next few months – it might save his life!

Kidney trouble

One of the most common serious diseases suffered by older cats is kidney failure. It tends to creep up on cats as they enter their teens (or 60s in human terms), causing gradual weight loss, dull coat, increased urination and drinking and general depression. Other symptoms can include vomiting, bad breath and a reduced appetite.

The diagnosis of kidney failure is made using a blood test, and once the disease has been confirmed, your vet will be able to advise on how best to treat and care for your cat to maximise his healthy life. Here are my top tips for looking after a cat with kidney failure:

Chicken and fish are great for cats with bad kidneys

These are the meats that cats can digest most easily, and which do the least amount of damage to the kidneys. So plenty of home-cooked chicken and white fish is great, and avoid cat foods with beef or lamb in them as much as possible.

Prescription diets can work wonders

Along with home-cooked meals, you should feed your cat on a special diet from your vet, containing exactly the right balance of nutrients including reduced phosphorus and increased potassium.

Less is more!

Protein is vital for cats – but too much can make cats with kidney disease feel really ill. Prescription diets and those aimed for older cats are ideal as they will have restricted protein levels.

Any food is better than no food

If your cat with kidney trouble is refusing to eat his new, healthy diet, don't worry too much. It's much better that he eats something, even if it is high protein and full of red meat. Just do your best to slip as much healthy chicken and fish into his bowl as you can get away with!

The 'scrawny dustbin' cat

For a while now you've noticed a change in your cat. Whereas he used to be content with a few meals a day, now he's constantly waiting by the food bowl, meowing loudly all day. Any food gets wolfed down in seconds but seems to do nothing to reduce his hunger. And despite all this eating, he seems to be losing weight really quickly – and getting really grumpy and irritable. What could be wrong with him?

If this sounds like your old cat then I've got some good news for you – he's probably suffering from a condition called 'hyperthyroidism' and it is relatively easy to cure. 'Hyperthyroidism' means an overactive thyroid gland. This gland controls the rate at which the body uses energy – a bit like the accelerator in a car – and hyperthyroid cats have swollen thyroid glands which make them burn energy at a massive rate. This causes the classic symptoms of weight loss despite massive hunger. Thankfully, it's quite straightforward to sort out. Once the disease has been confirmed with blood tests, your vet can use tablets to control the condition, or he may choose to remove the offending thyroid gland all together. Whatever treatment option you go for, the outlook is really good – which is great for your cat, and for your cat food bills!

Fluids are vital

To avoid complications it is really crucial to keep your cat fully hydrated, so make sure he gets fresh, preferably bottled, water every day.

Regular vet checks

Your vet will probably prescribe some tablets to help your cat's kidneys and schedule regular revisits to check up on his progress.

Diabetes

This is another common disease of older cats, and the symptoms are very similar to those experienced by people with diabetes: weight loss, increased appetite, increased thirst and increased urination. Your vet will diagnose the disease using blood and urine tests, and treatment usually involves twice daily injections of insulin (much easier and less stressful than it sounds!) and strict dietary management.

The dreaded 'C' word

Cancer is sadly all too common in older cats, and it's one of the biggest causes of death. There are many different forms of this disease, but in older cats tumours in the abdomen are probably the most common. Symptoms can be varied, but watch out for a gradual decline and loss of appetite associated with diarrhoea and vomiting. If you have any suspicions ask your vet to check the cat over as an early diagnosis does sometimes mean there is the possibility of surgical treatment to remove the cancer.

The final days

When the time comes it's important not to let your beloved old companion suffer for any longer than necessary. With the guidance of your vet, make your decision only when you know for sure that there is no hope of a recovery and that he really isn't having any quality of life. When a very elderly or ill cat refuses food for many days or weeks, and fails to respond to your voice or touch, and is too weak to move from his bed, it could be an indication that he's ready to go. Your vet will help you through this difficult time, and then, when you are both 100% sure, he or she will help him on his way. It's a totally painless injection and usually a great release for both cat and owner.

9. When Cat-astrophe Strikes!

From disagreements with cars to tumbling out of trees, cats are always getting into some kind of trouble. Most of the time they use up one of their nine lives, dust themselves off and carry on as if nothing has happened. However, occasionally they're not so lucky and end up in serious trouble. To help your cat effectively, it is vital to know what to do in this situation – so check out these key tips for dealing with a feline emergency:

Be prepared!

Just like the Boy Scouts, all good cat owners should be prepared for every emergency. Make sure you know the contact details of your vet, including the out-of-hours number and address, and have a small first aid kit which should include sterile dressings, bandages and antiseptic cream.

Check the vital five

If you're worried about your cat, check these five things before you panic:

1. Is he alert and bright?
2. Is he breathing normally?
3. Is he free from obvious injuries and bleeding?
4. Is the colour of his gums nice and pink?
5. Is his temperature normal?

If you've answered 'no' to any of these points, it's time to head to your vet for a check up, as there could be something wrong.

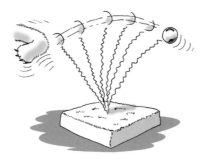

Road Traffic Accidents (RTA's) – the tell-tale signs to look out for:

If your cat has been hit by a car, these are the common symptoms to look for:

- Scuffed and broken claws – nails are often damaged as the cat is thrown across the tarmac and tries to dig his nails in.
- Obvious lameness.
- Blood or open wounds.
- Laboured breathing.

The injured cat action plan

If your cat has obviously been injured, whether through an RTA or other accident, there are several key things to remember when deciding what to do:

1. Keep him indoors to make sure he doesn't disappear off and hide somewhere.

2. Call your vet for immediate advice, and to let them know to expect you at the surgery.

3. Identify any obvious bleeding and apply pressure with a bandage if possible.

4. Offer water to drink but no food in case he needs an anaesthetic.

5. Wrap him in an old towel or blanket to restrain him and keep him warm.

6. Move him gently to a cat basket and head straight to the vet.

Cars vs cats

Being hit by a car is, unfortunately, an all-to-common cause of serious injury and death in cats. The best tip is to do everything you can to prevent your cat from being the victim of an RTA in the first place. Here are my five ways of keeping you cat safe from the roads:

1. Don't buy a house near a main road if you own a cat – or get a cat if you live near a main road!
2. Never let your cat out of the front door if it leads directly onto a road – make sure he comes and goes straight into the garden.
3. Fit him with a reflective collar that will shine brightly in a car's headlights.
4. If your garden borders a busy road, put up fencing or prickly bushes to try to prevent him wandering out onto the road.
5. Neuter him or her at an early age as this reduces the desire to wander.

Ears are easier. . .

A quick tip - to check your cat's temperature, buy yourself a child's thermometer designed for the ear. Simply follow the instructions and take his temperature from the ear rather than the other end…it's much more pleasant for all involved!

How to sort out a blocked cat!

I'm not talking about cats with writer's block – this is a tip for a much more serious condition often referred to as 'blocked cat syndrome' where they are unable to pass urine due to a blockage in the pipes (its real name is Feline Lower Urinary Tract Syndrome, or FLUTS). The blockage is caused by sludge and crystals in the bladder forming a plug in the urethra (the pipe to the outside world). When this happens, the bladder quickly fills up with urine, and unless the situation is sorted out, the consequences can quickly be life-threatening.

Here's how to spot a blocked cat:

- A male cat who is constantly squatting and straining to pass urine but very little is coming out.
- Licking around the back end.
- Crying out in pain.

If you suspect your cat might be blocked, get him straight down to the vet A.S.A.P. Here your vet will be able to unblock him using a special catheter, and might keep him in for observation for a few days to make sure the condition doesn't recur.

How to keep him unblocked!

Once your cat has had FLUTS he's likely to have a recurrence unless you take steps to prevent it. Here are my top tips for keeping him nice and unblocked!

- Make sure he drinks plenty of water – get him a water fountain which encourages him to drink, and offer him rainwater or bottled water instead of tap water.

- Give him mainly wet food, so plenty of home-cooked chicken and fish as well as pouches and tinned foods.

- Any dried food he eats should be special prescription food to reduce the crystals in his urine – ask your vet for details.

- Try to get his weight down if he is a fat cat.

Aspirin can be a life-saver

Old cats can get a really nasty condition where a blood clot blocks the main arteries to one or both back legs. This causes intense pain, and the typical symptoms include a complete loss of use of the back legs, which are cold to the touch. If you strongly suspect this condition there is something you can do immediately while you organise to get to the vet – give her half a junior aspirin. This may help dissolve the blood clot and could save her life – just make sure you let your vet know as it is easy to overdose cats with aspirin.

Take care with painkillers

While we're on the subject of aspirin, a quick word of warning if you are thinking of using aspirin or any other human painkiller for your cat if they have an injury or illness – don't! Aspirin can easily build up to dangerous levels in cats, and should never be given more frequently than once every two days, and paracetamol is really poisonous to cats and should never be given to them. If your cat needs pain relief, it's much better to consult your vet who can prescribe safe painkillers specially designed for cats.

A Brief History of the Cat

Wild at heart!

Every cat lover admires the big cats. Watching a nature film, the similarity between lions or tigers and our own domesticated kitties is often striking. We can readily recognize the walk, the facial expressions, the hunting technique (if only from watching our cats chase toys), and many other behavioural patterns.

That these great predators are members of the same family as the domestic cat is only too obvious. In fact all modern cats, wild or domestic, have one common ancestor - the miacids - which walked on this planet some tens of millions of years ago. A more direct ancestor, *Felis lunesis*, appeared on the stage twelve million years ago, and it is assumed that all modern small cats evolved from that prehistoric species.

Domestication

It seems that the first cats to live near people were the African wild cats of Egypt. These cats were probably attracted by the mice and rats that filled the Egyptian grain stores. Apparently, the ancient Egyptians were very appreciative of the cats' help in vermin control. In fact, they worshipped their cats and gave them a central place in their culture. The cats were considered gods and killing a cat was punishable by death.

It is believed that cats were introduced into Europe by Mediterranean traders. It is possible that cats also followed the trade routes all over the world, proving, as they migrated, to be invaluable in their role as vermin exterminators.

European Legacy

The cats that inhabited Europe during the Middle Ages endured serious persecution. The mysterious cat, with its superior senses and physical ability, was often seen as having a diabolic character. The close companionship between cats and elderly solitary women sometimes led to accusations of witchcraft - both women and cats suffered from the consequences.

Modern Times

As the Middle Ages came to an end, the popularity of the cat increased again in Europe and all over the world. Cats became admired pets once more and this time not necessarily for their hunting skills. New exotic breeds were imported to Britain from all over the empire, and the nineteenth century saw a rising interest in the breeding and showing of purebred cats. The first official cat show was held in 1871 in London's Crystal Palace.

During the twentieth century, and in particular from the 1950s, cats became even more cherished and loved. With its ability to adjust to the new living conditions in the growing urbanization of the modern world, the cat is now one of the most popular pets in the world. In the United States and in Europe it is estimated that cats are now more popular than dogs as household pets.

The quality of life of domesticated cats is also rising. Scientific research contributes to the creation of improved food and medical treatment, and also to a better understanding of feline behaviour. In a protected environment, cats today can reach old age and can enjoy a protective and mutually satisfying relationship with humans.

Unfortunately, the cat's ability to survive in harsh conditions has also created a serious problem of overpopulation. Too many cats end their lives as strays and feral cats struggling for a meagre existence, or at animal shelters. It is our duty as cat owners to take care of this situation. If we prevent the birth of unwanted kittens, then in the long-run most cats will have good homes. Only then can we truly say that the cat's story has reached a happy stage in the twenty-first century.

Cat Trivia

Did you know. . .

- Both humans and cats have identical regions in the brain responsible for emotion.

- A cat's brain is more similar to a man's brain than that of a dog!

- A cat has more bones than a human; humans have 206, but an adult cat has 230 (kittens have 245 bones, but some fuse together as the cat ages).

- Cats have 30 vertebrae - 5 more than humans.

- Cats do not have a collarbone, so they can fit through any opening the size of their head.

- Cats have 32 muscles that control the outer ear (compared to human's 6 muscles each). A cat can rotate its ears independently 180º, and can turn them in the direction of sound 10 times faster than those of the best watchdog.

- A cat's hearing rates as one of the top in the animal kingdom. Cats can hear sounds as high-pitched as 65 kHz; a human's hearing stops at just 20 kHz.

- In relation to their body size, cats have the largest eyes of any mammal.

- Most cats do not have eyelashes.

- A cat sees about 6 times better than a human at night, and needs 1/6 the amount of light that a human does - it has a layer of extra reflecting cells which absorb light.

- Cats can see up to 120' away and their peripheral vision is about 285º.

- Blue-eyed, white cats are often deaf.

- Cats have about 100 different vocalisation sounds. In comparison, dogs have about 10.

- Cats have better memories than dogs. Tests conducted by the University of Michigan concluded that while a dog's memory lasts no more than 5 minutes, a cat's can last as long as 16 hours - exceeding even that of monkeys and orang-utans.

- A cat has approximately 60 to 80 million 'smell' cells in its nose (a human has between 5 and 20 million).

- Cats have a special scent organ located in the roof of their mouth, called the Jacobson's organ. It analyses smells - and is the reason why you will sometimes see your cat "sneer" when they encounter a strong odour.

- A cat has a total of 24 whiskers, 4 rows of whiskers on each side. The upper two rows can move independently of the bottom two rows. A cat uses its whiskers for measuring distances.

- Cats have 30 teeth (12 incisors, 10 premolars, 4 canines, and 4 molars), while dogs have 42. Kittens have baby teeth, which are replaced by permanent teeth around the age of 7 months.

- When a cat drinks, its tongue - which has tiny barbs on it - scoops the liquid up backwards.

- Domestic cats purr both when inhaling and when exhaling.

- Cats step with both left legs, then both right legs when they walk or run.

- Cats are the only animals to walk on their toes rather than the base of their feet.

- A domestic cat can sprint at about 31 miles per hour.

- The heaviest cat on record weighed 46 lbs.
- A kitten will typically weigh about 3 oz at birth. The typical male housecat will weigh between 7 and 9 pounds, slightly less for female housecats.
- Cats take between 20-40 breaths per minute.
- Normal body temperature for a cat is 102º F.
- A cat's normal pulse is 140-240 beats per minute, with an average of 195.
- Cats' urine glows under ultraviolet light.
- A female cat flea can eat fifteen times its own weight every day!
- Cats lose almost as much fluid in the saliva while grooming themselves as they do through urination.
- Almost 10% of a cat's bones are in its tail, and the tail is used to maintain balance.
- The domestic cat is the only species able to hold its tail vertically while walking. You can also learn about your cat's present state of mind by observing the *posture* of his tail.
- If a cat is frightened, the hair stands up fairly evenly all over the body; when the cat threatens or is ready to attack, the hair stands up only in a narrow band along the spine and tail.
- The first true cats came into existence about 12 million years ago.

- Phoenician cargo ships are thought to have brought the first domesticated cats to Europe in about 900 BC.
- The ancient Egyptians were the first to tame the cat (in about 3000 BC), and used them to control pests. Killing a cat was a crime punishable by death.
- Ancient Egyptian family members shaved their eyebrows in mourning when the family cat died. They also made mummies of cats, and embalmed mice were placed with them in their tombs. In one ancient city, over 300,000 cat mummies were found.
- In Siam, the cat was so revered that one rode in a chariot at the head of a parade celebrating the new king.
- The first breeding pair of Siamese cats arrived in England in 1884.
- The first formal cat show in the world was held in England in 1871.
- There are approximately 100 breeds of cat.
- The life expectancy of cats has nearly doubled since 1930 - from 8 to 16 years.
- Cats respond most readily to names that end in an "ee" sound.
- A female cat will be pregnant for approximately 9 weeks - between 62 and 65 days from conception to delivery.
- Female felines are "superfecund", which means that each of the kittens in her litter can have a different father.

- Many cats love having their forehead gently stroked.
- If a cat is frightened, put your hand over its eyes and forehead, or let him bury his head in your armpit to help calm him.
- A cat will tremble or shiver when it is in extreme pain.
- Cats should not be fed tuna exclusively, as it lacks taurine, an essential nutrient required for good feline health.
- Purring does not always indicate that a cat is happy and healthy - some cats will purr loudly when they are terrified or in pain.
- Not every cat gets "high" from catnip. If the cat doesn't have a specific gene (and about 20% don't), it won't react. Catnip is non-addictive.
- Cats must have fat in their diet because they can't produce it on their own.
- While many cats enjoy milk, it will give some cats diarrhoea.
- A cat will spend nearly 30% of her life grooming herself.
- A cat's mother will teach it to hunt and kill. If a kitten isn't taught by its natural mother the chances are that it probably won't know what to do with prey when it has caught it!
- When a domestic cat goes after mice, about 1 pounce in 3 results in a catch.
- On average a mature, healthy cat spends only 35% of its life awake, or roughly 6-8 hours a day. Cats come back to full alertness faster than any other creature.

- A cat can jump 5 times as high as it is tall. In comparison a human would have to jump 29'!

- The average lifespan of an outdoor-only cat (feral and non-feral) is about 3 years; an indoor-only cat can live 16 years and longer.

- Cats with long, lean bodies are more likely to be outgoing, and more protective and vocal than those with a stocky build.

- Most cats adore sardines.

- It has been scientifically proven that stroking a cat can lower your own blood pressure.

- If your cat snores, or rolls over on his back to expose his belly, it means he trusts you.

- Cats respond better to women than to men, probably due to the fact that women's voices have a higher pitch.

- When your cat rubs up against you, she is actually marking you as "hers" with her scent. If your cat pushes his face against your head, it is a sign of acceptance and affection.

- Contrary to popular belief, people are not allergic to cat fur, dander, saliva, or urine - they are allergic to "sebum", a fatty substance secreted by the cat's sebaceous glands. It has been shown that male cats secrete much greater amounts of this allergen than females. A neutered male sheds much less than a non-neutered male.

- Cat bites are more likely to become infected than dog bites.

- Napoleon Bonaparte, Dwight D. Eisenhower and Adolf Hitler all had ailurophobia, or a fear of cats.

- Cat litter was "invented" in 1947 when Edward Lowe asked his neighbour to try dried, granulated clay used to sop up grease spills in factories. (In 1990, Mr. Lowe sold his business for over £100 million.)

- Cats lived with soldiers in trenches, where they killed mice, during World War I.

- The cat appears to be the only domestic animal not mentioned in the Bible.

- Sir Isaac Newton invented the cat-flap.

THE BLUE CROSS
Britain's pet charity

Britain's Pet Charity

The Blue Cross has been providing practical support, information and advice for pet and horse owners for over 100 years. Through a network of 11 animal adoption centres it re-homes thousands of dogs, cats, small animals and horses every year. Many of the animals the charity takes in are unwanted, some are strays and a few are much-loved pets whose owners have passed away. Whatever the animal's background, The Blue Cross works hard to match each animal to the right owner, resulting in permanent loving homes.

The charity also has four animal hospitals that provide veterinary treatment for the pets of people who cannot afford private vets' fees. Two equine centres rehabilitate horses before finding them suitable homes on a loan scheme, and the charity's third equine centre will open in 2006.

The Blue Cross receives no government funding and so relies entirely on donations from the public. It has a growing nationwide network of trained volunteers, who speak to classes of children in primary schools and in youth groups. The speakers teach the children empathy, interaction with and behaviour around animals. The Blue Cross also provides the Pet Bereavement Support Service (PBSS), where experienced volunteers give support to those dealing with the loss of a pet.

To find out more about the charity, including animals for adoption, the programme of fundraising events and how to volunteer, please visit www.bluecroos.org.uk call 01993 825500, or email info@bluecross.org.uk.

Don't lose a loved one!

Did you know over 3,000 cats go missing in Britain every week? To prevent the worst from happening to your cat, it is a good idea to have them registered with a pet reunification service.

The Missing Pets Bureau has nearly 100,000 pets registered nationwide and is the UK's leading pet reunification service. With cats so prone to stray, that extra security, and peace of mind, is worth having!

With the service, you get a unique Petback ID tag linked to specialist support services open 24 hours a day, 365 days a year. If your cat ever goes missing - even on Christmas Day - the team will work day and night to get them back; placing their details on the national Missing Pets Register and putting word out among a network of 12,000 pet care organisations nationwide.

If someone finds your cat, they will contact the Missing Pets Bureau using the freephone number on the back of your cat's Petback ID tag and the Missing Pets Bureau will contact you immediately on one of four numbers – including an emergency number. This not only protects your identity but also ensures a safe, speedy recovery of your loved one.

There are two types of protection you can go for: Petback Protect or Petback MedAlert. The MedAlert service has the added benefit of providing assistance if your cat if it has been involved in an accident while missing. Don't lose a loved one! Call the Missing Pets Bureau today on freephone 0800 0195 123 or visit their website at www.missingpetsbureau.com.

Index

Index

Index

R

Rescue cats, *14*
Roundworms, *48, 61*
Rubbing, *111*

S

Scratching, *69, 71*
Sex chromosomes, *39*
Siamese, *15, 37*
Skin cancer, *72*
Stray cats, *12*
Stress, *111*
Sunburn, *72*
Sunscreen, *72*
Supreme Cat Show, *18*
Symptoms, *112*

T

Tantrums, *74, 75*
Tapeworms, *48, 61*
Taurine, *88*
Teeth care, *108-110*
Temperature, taking, *133*
Territory, *77, 78, 84*
The Blue Cross, *14, 148*
The Missing Pets Bureau, *50, 149*
Toilet training, *42, 44, 84*
Tortoiseshell cats, *39*
Trivia, *141-147*

U

Urinating, *84, 121*
Urinary blockage, *134*

V

Vaccinations, *45, 47, 48, 53*
Vet, *45, 112*
Vomiting, *105, 121, 127*

W

Water, *99, 107*
Weight loss, *121*
Whiskers, *72, 80*
Worms / worming, *19, 45, 48, 53, 61-64, 105*

Notes

Notes

Notes

'The Greatest Tips in the World' series . . .

Also available:

ISBN 1-905151-02-0
Pub Date: Sept 2005

ISBN 1-905151-03-9
Pub Date: Sept 2005

ISBN 1-905151-04-7
Pub Date: Sept 2005

ISBN 1-905151-05-5
Pub Date: Sept 2005

ISBN 1-905151-06-3
Pub Date: Oct 2004

ISBN 1-905151-09-8
Pub Date: April 2006

ISBN 1-905151-08-X
Pub Date: April 2006

ISBN 1-905151-07-1
Pub Date: April 2006

ISBN 1-905151-11-X
Pub Date: Sept 2006

ISBN 1-905151-12-8
Pub Date: Sept 2006

ISBN 1-905151-13-6
Pub Date: Sept 2006

With many more to follow, these books will form a most useful compilation for any bookshelf.

Other 'The Greatest in the World' products . . .

DVDs

'The Greatest Gardening Tips in the World' - presented by Steve Brookes
(release date: September 2005)

'The Greatest Cat Tips in the World' - presented by Joe Inglis
(release date: September 2006)

'The Greatest Dog Tips in the World' - presented by Joe Inglis
(release date: September 2006)

'The Greatest Golfing Tips in the World' - Vols. 1 & 2 - presented by
John Cook (release date: September 2006)

'The Greatest Yoga Tips in the World' - presented by David Gellineau and
David Robson (release date: September 2005)

'The Greatest Cat Cuisine in the World' - presented by Joe Inglis
(release date: September 2006)

'The Greatest Dog Cusine in the World' - presented by Joe Inglis
(release date: September 2006)

Hardback, full-colour books:

'The Greatest Cat Cuisine in the World' - by Joe Inglis
ISBN 1-905151-14-4 (publication date: September 2006)

'The Greatest Dog Cuisine in the World' - by Joe Inglis
ISBN 1-905151-15-2 (publication date: September 2006)

For more information about currently available and forthcoming book and
DVD titles please visit:

www.thegreatestintheworld.com

or write to:
Public Eye Publications
PO Box 3182
Stratford-upon-Avon
Warwickshire CV37 7XW
United Kingdom

Tel / Fax: +44(0)1789 299616
Email: info@publiceyepublications.co.uk

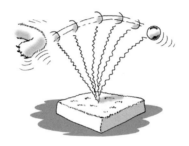